Black and Purple and Gold Football Poetry Memory Book

Black and Purple and Gold Football Poetry Memory Book

Walter the Educator

Silent King Books
a WhichHead Entertainment Imprint

Copyright © 2024 by Walter the Educator

All rights reserved. No part of this book may be reproduced in any manner whatsoever without written permission except in the case of brief quotations embodied in critical articles and reviews.

First Printing, 2024

Disclaimer

This book is a literary work; the story is not about specific persons, teams, games, locations, situations, and/or circumstances unless mentioned in a historical context. Any resemblance to real persons, teams, games, locations, situations, and/or circumstances is coincidental. This book is for entertainment and informational purposes only. The author and publisher offer this information without warranties expressed or implied. No matter the grounds, neither the author nor the publisher will be accountable for any losses, injuries, or other damages caused by the reader's use of this book. The use of this book acknowledges an understanding and acceptance of this disclaimer.

Black and Purple and Gold Football Poetry Memory Book is a memory book that belongs to the Sports Poetry Memory Book Series by Walter the Educator. Collect them all and more books at WaltertheEducator.com.

USE THE EXTRA SPACE TO DOCUMENT YOUR FOOTBALL MEMORIES THROUGHOUT THE YEARS

This little collectible keepsake book belongs to

_____

Beneath the sky, both bold and bright,

The colors rise, a radiant sight,

Black as the storm that fierce winds bring,

Purple like twilight, where dreams take wing.

And Gold, the sun's last mighty glow,

A beacon strong, to lead and show.

The field is set, the banners wave,

Black and Purple, strong and brave,

A tale of grit in every thread,

Of victories won, and futures led.

The helmets glisten, armor tight,

In Black, they stand, prepared for fight.

Purple roars, a regal hue,

A clash of wills, the hearts stay true.

Beneath this shade of twilight's fall,

They charge ahead, they rise, stand tall.

For in the shadows where others fade,

They thrive, they battle, unafraid.

And Gold, it shines, a timeless crown,

For every triumph, for each renown.

It speaks of honor, speaks of pride,

It's more than just a gleaming guide.

It's sweat and tears, a shining crest,

A symbol of their very best.

The Black: relentless, pure as night,

It cloaks their fears, it fuels the fight.

It whispers strength in every play,

The dark, the force that clears the way.

Through hardship, toil, and unknown fears,

The Black endures, it never veers.

The Purple: rich, like royalty's claim,

It holds the heart, it frames the game.

Like twilight skies before the dawn,

It signals hope, a promise drawn.

When moments grow, both fierce and still,

Purple stands as strength of will.

The Gold: it calls, a brighter light,

A gleam that cuts the deepest night.

For every goal, for every win,

It tells the story from within.

ABOUT THE CREATOR

Walter the Educator is one of the pseudonyms for Walter Anderson. Formally educated in Chemistry, Business, and Education, he is an educator, an author, a diverse entrepreneur, and he is the son of a disabled war veteran. "Walter the Educator" shares his time between educating and creating. He holds interests and owns several creative projects that entertain, enlighten, enhance, and educate, hoping to inspire and motivate you. Follow, find new works, and stay up to date with Walter the Educator™

at WaltertheEducator.com

Milton Keynes UK
Ingram Content Group UK Ltd.
UKHW020740071024
449371UK00014B/961